AVOCADO–BASED
COOKBOOK

**58 SIMPLE AND NATURAL WAYS TO
ADD MORE POTASSIUM TO YOUR DIET THROUGH
DELICIOUS RECIPES THAT WILL
MAKE YOU LOVE THIS SUPERFOOD.**

By
Aimie Lee

CONTENTS

INTRODUCTION

Scientific studies point out that American diets are deficient in fruit, vegetables, whole grains and dairy products. These foods are essential as they are rich in potassium, calcium, dietary fibre and vitamin D. Therefore, it is crucial to compensate for these deficiencies by eating foods that contain these nutritional values.

Potassium and sodium are electrolytes needed by the body to function normally and help maintain fluids and blood volume in the body. When we sweat, we also lose water and electrolytes (i.e. 'salts' such as sodium, chloride, potassium). Drinking enough water and having enough electrolytes is necessary for our bodies to function correctly.

The body needs to replace the electrolytes it loses through sweating. Potassium is an electrolyte that helps muscles contract and regulates the balance of fluids and minerals in and out of body cells. Low potassium intake can increase the risk of disease and may involve hypertension and stroke, kidney stones, bone health, blood sugar control and type 2 diabetes.

There is potassium in vegetables, fruits (such as avocados), seafood and dairy products.

With just 50g of avocado, you get 6% of your daily potassium requirement.

Potassium is essential because it is responsible for the proper functioning of the nerves, heart and kidneys and can also reduce cardiovascular diseases, such as heart disease and stroke, by lowering blood pressure.

A diet rich in potassium can offset some of the adverse effects of sodium on blood pressure.

Avocados are also a good source of essential nutrients such as fibre, folate, vitamin K, pantothenic acid and copper.

Taking potassium is vital for balanced blood pressure, proper kidney and heart function, supporting muscular muscle contraction and smooth nerve transmission.

Increased blood pressure is caused by:

- Excessive sodium
- Insufficient potassium intake
- Overweight and obesity
- Excessive alcohol consumption

Potassium can make you thinner and lower the harmful effects of sodium on blood pressure.

Other possible benefits of a potassium-rich diet include:

- Reduced risk of developing kidney stones
- Decreased bone loss

The dietary guidelines also state that the adequate intake (AI) for potassium is as follows:

- Adult men 19+ years -3,400 mg per day;
- Mature women 19+ years 2,600 mg per day.

AIs are amounts of a nutrient that are adequate for almost everyone in the population; therefore, intakes below an AI may also be acceptable for some people.

If you're looking for different ways to add avocado to your diet, try my 58 tasty avocado recipes that will make you love this super fruit.

CHAPTER 1

THE HEALTH BENEFITS OF AVOCADO

The avocado is a rather unique fruit.

While most fruit consists primarily of carbohydrate, avocado is high in healthy fats.

Numerous studies show that it has powerful health benefits and here are 12 health benefits of avocado that are supported by scientific research.

1. AVOCADO IS INCREDIBLY NUTRITIOUS

Avocado is the fruit of the avocado tree, scientifically known as Persea Americana. Avocado is a green, pear-shaped fruit often called an "alligator pear." It is loaded with healthy fats, fiber and various important nutrients.

This fruit is prized for its high nutrient value and is added to various dishes due to its good flavor and rich texture. It is the main ingredient in guacamole.

These days, the avocado has become an incredibly popular food among health-conscious individuals. It's often referred to as a super food, which is not surprising given its health properties.

There are many types of avocado that vary in shape and color — from pear-shaped to round and green to black. They can also weigh anywhere from 8 ounces (220 grams) to 3 pounds (1.4 kg).

The most popular variety is the Hass avocado.

The yellow-green flesh inside the fruit is eaten, but the skin and seed are discarded.

Avocados are very nutritious and contain a wide variety of nutrients, including 20 different vitamins and minerals.

Here are some of the most abundant nutrients, in a single 3.5-ounce serving:

Vitamin K: 26% of the daily value (DV)
Folate: 20% of the DV
Vitamin C: 17% of the DV

Potassium: 14% of the DV
Vitamin B5: 14% of the DV
Vitamin B6: 13% of the DV
Vitamin E: 10% of the DV

It also contains small amounts of magnesium, manganese, copper, iron, zinc, phosphorous and vitamins A, B1 (thiamine), B2 (riboflavin) and B3 (niacin).

This is coming with 160 calories, 2 grams of protein and 15 grams of healthy fats. Although it contains 9 grams of carbs, 7 of those are fiber, so there are only 2 net carbs, making this a low-carb friendly plant food.

Avocados do not contain any cholesterol or sodium and are low in saturated fat. This is why they are favored by some experts who believe these substances are harmful, which is a debated topic, however.

This is coming with 160 calories, 2 grams of protein and 15 grams of healthy fats. Although it contains 9 grams of carbs, 7 of those are fiber, so there are only 2 net carbs, making this a low-carb friendly plant food.

Avocados do not contain any cholesterol or sodium and are low in saturated fat. This is why they are favored by some experts who believe these substances are harmful, which is a debated topic, however.

2. AVOCADO CONTAIN MORE POTASSIUM THAN BANANAS

Potassium is a nutrient that most people don't get enough of.

This nutrient helps maintain electrical gradients in your body's cells and serves various important functions.

Avocados are very high in potassium. A 3.5-ounce (100-gram) serving packs 14% of the recommended daily allowance (RDA), compared to 10% in bananas, which are a typical high-potassium food.

3. AVOCADO IS LOADED WITH HEART-HEALTHY MONOUNSATURATED FATTY ACIDS

Avocados and avocado oil are high in monounsaturated oleic acid, a heart-healthy fatty acid that is believed to be one of the main reasons for the health benefits of olive oil.

Avocado is a high-fat food.

In fact, 77% of the calories in it are from fat, making it one of the fattiest plant foods in existence.

But they don't just contain any fat. The majority of the fat in avocado is oleic acid — a monounsaturated fatty acid that is also the major component of olive oil and believed to be responsible for some of its health benefits.

Oleic acid has been associated with reduced inflammation and shown to have beneficial effects on genes linked to cancer. The fats in avocado are also rather resistant to heat-induced oxidation, making avocado oil a healthy and safe choice for cooking.

4. AVOCADO ARE LOADED WITH FIBER

Avocados tend to be rich in fiber — about 7% by weight, which is very high compared to most other foods. Fiber may have important benefits for weight loss and metabolic health.

Fiber is another nutrient that avocados are relatively rich in.

It's indigestible plant matter that can contribute to weight loss, reduce blood sugar spikes and is strongly linked to a lower risk of many diseases. A distinction is often made between soluble and insoluble fiber.

Soluble fiber is known for feeding the friendly gut bacteria in your intestine, which are very important for optimal body function.

A 3.5-ounce (100-gram) serving of avocado packs 7 grams of fiber, which is 27% of the RDA.

About 25% of the fiber in avocado is soluble, while 75% is insoluble.

5. EATING AVOCADOS CAN LOWER CHOLESTEROL AND TRIGLYCERIDES LEVELS

Numerous studies have shown that eating avocado can improve heart disease risk factors like total, "bad" LDL and "good" HDL cholesterol, as well as blood triglycerides.

Heart disease is the most common cause of death in the world.

It's known that several blood markers are linked to an increased risk.

This includes cholesterol, triglycerides, inflammatory markers, blood pressure and various others.

Eight controlled studies in people have examined the effects of avocado on some of these risk factors.

These studies showed that avocados can:

- Reduce total cholesterol levels significantly.
- Reduce blood triglycerides by up to 20%.
- Lower LDL cholesterol by up to 22%.
- Increase HDL (the good) cholesterol by up to 11%.

One of the studies found that including avocado in a low-fat, vegetarian diet significantly improved the cholesterol profile.

Though their results are impressive, it's important to note that all of the human studies were small and short-term, including only 13–37 people with duration of 1–4 weeks.

6. PEOPLE WHO EAT AVOCADOS TEND TO BE HEALTHIER

One dietary survey found that people who ate avocados had a much higher nutrient intake and a lower risk of metabolic syndrome.

One study looked at the dietary habits and health of people who eat avocados.

They analyzed data from 17,567 participants in the NHANES survey in the US.

Avocado consumers were found to be much healthier than people who didn't eat this fruit.

They had a much higher nutrient intake and were half as likely to have metabolic syndrome, a cluster of symptoms that are a major risk factor for heart disease and diabetes.

People who ate avocados regularly also weighed less, had a lower BMI and significantly less belly fat. They also had higher levels of "good" HDL cholesterol.

However, correlation does not imply causation, and there is no guarantee that the avocados caused these people to be in better health.

Therefore, this particular study doesn't carry much weight.

7. THEIR FAT CONTENT MAY HELP YOU ABSORB NUTRIENTS FROM PLANT FOODS

Studies have shown that eating avocado or avocado oil with vegetables can dramatically increase the number of antioxidants you take in.

When it comes to nutrients, your intake is not the only thing that matters.

You also need to be able to absorb these nutrients — move them from your digestive tract and to your body, where they can be used.

Some nutrients are fat-soluble, meaning that they need to be combined with fat in order to be utilized.

Vitamins A, D, E and K are fat-soluble, along with antioxidants like carotenoids.

One study showed that adding avocado or avocado oil to either salad or salsa can increase antioxidant absorption 2.6- to 15-fold.

So, not only is avocado highly nutritious, it can dramatically increase the nutrient value of other plant foods that you are eating.

This is an excellent reason to always include a healthy fat source when you eat veggies. Without it, a lot of the beneficial plant nutrients will go to waste.

8. AVOCADOS ARE LOADED WITH POWERFUL ANTIOXIDANTS THAT CAN PROTECT YOUR EYES

Avocados are high in antioxidants, including lutein and zeaxanthin. These nutrients are very important for eye health and lower your risk of macular degeneration and cataracts.

Not only do avocados increase antioxidant absorption from other foods, they are also high in antioxidants themselves.

This includes the carotenoids lutein and zeaxanthin, which are incredibly important for eye health.

Studies show that they're linked to a drastically reduced risk of cataracts and macular degeneration, which are common in older adults.

Therefore, eating avocados should benefit your eye health over the long term.

9. AVOCADO MAY HELP PREVENT CANCER

Some test-tube studies have shown that nutrients in avocados may have benefits in preventing prostate cancer and lowering side effects of chemotherapy. However, human-based research is lacking.

There is limited evidence that avocado may be beneficial in cancer treatment and prevention.

Test-tube studies suggest that it may help reduce side effects of chemotherapy in human lymphocytes.

Avocado extract has also been shown to inhibit the growth of prostate cancer cells in a laboratory.

However, keep in mind that these studies were done in isolated cells and don't necessarily prove what may happen inside people. Human-based research is unavailable.

10. AVOCADO EXTRACT MAY HELP RELIEVE SYMPTOMS OF ARTHRITIS

Studies have shown that avocado and soybean oil extracts can significantly reduce symptoms of osteoarthritis.

Arthritis is a common problem in Western countries. There are many types of this condition, which are often chronic problems that people have for the rest of their lives.

Multiple studies suggest that avocado and soybean oil extracts — called avocado and soybean unsaponifiables — can reduce osteoarthritis.

Whether avocados themselves have this effect remains to be seen.

---

11. EATING AVOCADO MAY HELP YOU LOSE WEIGHT

Avocados may aid weight loss by keeping you full longer and making you eat fewer calories. They're also high in fiber and low in carbs, which may promote weight loss.

There is some evidence that avocados are a weight loss friendly food.

In one study, people eating avocado with a meal felt 23% more satisfied and had a 28% lower desire to eat over the next 5 hours, compared to people who did not consume this fruit.

Should this hold true in the long term, then including avocados in your diet may help you naturally eat fewer calories and make it easier for you to stick to healthy eating habits.

Avocados are also high in fiber and very low in carbs, two attributes that should help promote weight loss as well, at least in the context of a healthy, real-food-based diet.

12. AVOCADO IS DELICIOUS AND EASY TO INCORPORATE IN YOUR DIET

Avocados have a creamy, rich, fatty texture and blend well with other ingredients. Therefore, it's easy to add this fruit to your diet. Using lemon juice may prevent cut avocados from browning quickly.

Avocados are not only healthy; they're also incredibly delicious and go with many types of food.

You can add them to salads and various recipes or simply scoop them out with a spoon and eat them plain.

They have a creamy, rich, fatty texture and blend well with other ingredients.

A notable mention is guacamole, which is arguably the most famous use of avocados. It includes avocado along with ingredients like salt, garlic, lime and a few others depending on the recipe.

An avocado often takes some time to ripen and should feel slightly soft when ripe. The nutrients in avocado can oxidize and turn brown soon after fleshing it, but adding lemon juice should slow down this process.

CHAPTER 2

Breakfast Recipe

GREEN SMOOTHIE

SERVES: 2

01

TOTAL TIME: 5 MIN

DIRECTIONS:

Place all the ingredients in your blender. Blend until smooth. For a thinner smoothie, add a bit more almond milk.

INGREDIENTS:

1 LARGE BANANA RIPE, PEELED, SLICED

½ MEDIUM RIPE AVOCADO

½ ICEBERG LETTUCE

½ SCOOP PLAIN OF VANILLA PROTEIN POWDER

1/2 CUP ALMOND MILK

AVOCADO GINGER LATTE

Serves: 1

02

Total Time: 5 min

Directions:

Heat almond milk until warm and frothy.

Transfer to a blender with avocado and ginger. Blend well until frothy. You can also use an immersion blender to mix.

Strain latte through a fine mesh strainer (optional, but this ensures the smoothest consistency). Sip and enjoy.

Ingredients:

½ PIECE OF GINGER PEELED

½ SMASHED AVOCADO

1 CUP UNSWEETENED ALMOND MILK

	SERVES: 2	TOTAL TIME: 10 MIN
GREEN EGGS	03	

DIRECTIONS:	INGREDIENTS:
Spray a pan with oil and set over a medium-high heat. Add greens and cook, stirring, until just tender. in a bowl, combine eggs and parmesan. Add to pan and stir gently, until eggs are cooked. Serve eggs with toasted bread spread with avocado. Season with black pepper.	1 SPRAY OIL 1 ½ CUPS CHOPPED GREENS (KALETTES, SPINACH, BROCCOLI) 2 EGGS LIGHTLY BEATEN 1 TBSP. GRATED PARMESAN 1-2 SLICED GRAINY BREAD ¼ AVOCADO

BLUEBERRY AND AVOCADO MUFFINS

SERVES: 2

04

TOTAL TIME: 5 MIN

DIRECTIONS:

Preheat the oven to 375°F. Lightly spray a standard 12-cup muffin pan with cooking spray or line it with paper bake cups.

In a large bowl, stir together the avocado, sugar, milk, eggs, and vanilla.

In a medium bowl, stir together the flour, baking powder, ginger, and salt.

In two to three batches, stir the flour mixture into the avocado mixture until just combined but no flour is visible; don't over mix. Gently fold in the blueberries. Spoon the batter into the muffin cups.

Bake for 25 to 30 minutes, or until a wooden toothpick inserted in the

INGREDIENTS:

1 MEDIUM AVOCADO (HALVED, PITTED, MASHED WITH A FORK)

½ CUP SUGAR

½ CUP FAT FREE MILK

2 LARGE EGGS

1 TSP. VANILLA EXTRACT

2 CUPS ALL-PURPOSE FLOUR

4 TSPS. BAKING POWDER

1 TSP. GROUND GINGER

1/16 TSP. SALT

2 CUPS BLUEBERRIES

center comes out clean and the muffins are golden brown, turning the pan once after 15 minutes of baking time.

Transfer the pan to a cooling rack. Let stand for 5 minutes.

AVOCADO WAFFLES

SERVES: 6	TOTAL TIME: 25 MIN
05	

DIRECTIONS:

Prepare waffle iron with cooking spray and preheat.

Combine all dry ingredients in a bowl and mix well.

Combine all liquid ingredients, except whisked egg whites, together in the bowl of a stand mixer and mix until well combined.

In 1/2 cup additions, add dry ingredients to the liquid ingredients, combining well between additions until all dry ingredients are added.

Remove bowl from mixer and gently fold stiff egg whites into mixture until combined.

Let mixture rest 20 minutes.

Bake waffles and either serve traditionally with seasonal fruit and syrup or savory with a chunky avocado tomato salsa and a fried egg.

INGREDIENTS:

1 ½ CUP ALMOND FLOUR

½ CUP CORN STARCH

4 TSPS. BAKING POWDER

¼ TSP. KOSHER SALT

1 CUP BUTTERMILK

½ CUP MASHED AVOCADO

2 EGGS SEPARATED WHITES WHISKED UNTIL STIFF PEAKS FORM

1 TSP. PURE VANILLA EXTRACT

½ TSP. GROUND CINNAMON LEAVE OUT IF MAKING SAVORY WAFFLES

2 TSPS. COCONUT SUGAR OR MAPLE SYRUP OPTIONAL FOR SAVORY WAFFLES

AVOCADO OIL OR OTHER COOKING SPRAY

CHAPTER 3

Dips, Spreads Condiments

SHIITAKE BACON & EGG TACOS

	SERVES: 2	TOTAL TIME: 45 MIN
	06	

DIRECTIONS:

Make the Shiitake Bacon

Preheat the oven to 325°F and line a large baking sheet with parchment paper. Toss the shiitake mushrooms with the olive oil and tamari and toss to coat. Spread in an even layer on the baking sheet. Roast 30 to 40 minutes or until dark brown and lightly crisp around the edges. Set aside. (If you made your shiitake bacon in advance, warm it in the oven for a few minutes, if desired.)

Make the Cherry Tomato Pico:

In a small bowl, combine the tomatoes, onion, cilantro, lime juice, garlic, jalapeno and salt. Set aside.

When ready to serve, brush a medium nonstick stick skillet lightly with olive oil and bring to medium heat. Add the eggs, let them cook for a few seconds, and then stir and scramble until the eggs until just set.

INGREDIENTS:

SHIITAKE BACON

8 OUNCES SHIITAKE MUSHROOMS, STEMMED AND SLICED

2 TBSPS. EXTRA-VIRGIN OLIVE OIL

1 TBSP. TAMARI

CHERRY TOMATO PICO

1 CUP CHERRY OR GRAPE TOMATOES, SLICED IN HALF

¼ CUP FINELY DICED RED ONION

¼ CUP DICED CILANTRO

2 TBSPS. FRESH LIME JUICE

1 GARLIC CLOVE, MINCED

½ JALAPEÑO, STEMMED AND DICED

Assemble the tacos with the eggs, avocado slices, shiitake bacon, scoops of the cherry tomato Pico. Top with the micro greens and sliced Serranos and serve with lime wedges, if desired.

¼ Tsp. sea salt

For the Tacos

3 large eggs

Extra-virgin olive oil, for brushing

4 tortillas, charred or warmed

½ avocado, sliced

Micro greens, optional

Sliced serrano peppers, optional

Lime wedges, if desired, for serving

AVOCADO CREAM AND MINT CUCUMBERS

SERVES: 6	TOTAL TIME: 45 MIN
07	

DIRECTIONS:

Cut the upper cap of the avocados and scoop with a spoon; recover all the pulp leaving intact the «shells».

Put the empty avocado «shells» in the freezer for at least 30 minutes. Clean the spring onion, removing the green, and cut into small pieces. Peel the cucumbers, remove the seeds and cut into pieces.

Blend together avocado pulp, cucumbers and spring onion with a drop of water (increase the amount, if you prefer a more fluid consistency) and lime juice. Season it to taste with salt and add a few pieces of mint and chili. Cut the edge of the shells with scissors, to widen the mouth. Fill them with cream and serve on an ice bed.

INGREDIENTS:

6 AVOCADOS

2 CUCUMBERS

5 FILES

1 SPRING ONION

1 BUNCH OF MINT

1 CHILI PEPPER

¼ TSP. SALT AND PEPPER

AVOCADO MOUSSE

SERVES: 2-4	TOTAL TIME: 5 MIN
08	

DIRECTIONS:

Drain the ricotta cheese to remove the serum and make it dry.

Wash, cut and peel the avocado and remove all the pulp with a spoon.

Put the avocado pulp in the mixer and add the ricotta cheese, pepper, lemon juice and salt. You get a cream to serve.

INGREDIENTS:

1 AVOCADO

120 CUP OF RICOTTA CHEESE

1 TSP. LEMON JUICE

1/8 TSP. PEPPER AND SALT

THICK GUACAMOLE

	SERVES: 4	TOTAL TIME: 2-3H
	09	

DIRECTIONS:

Add the avocado to a bowl. Sprinkle with the lemon juice and toss gently to coat the avocado in the lemon juice.

Add the remaining ingredients and mix gently.

Cover the bowl and refrigerate for 2-3 hours or overnight. Mix gently before serving.

INGREDIENTS:

2 AVOCADOS, PEELED AND DICED

1 TBSP. FRESH-SQUEEZED LEMON JUICE

1 TOMATO, SEEDED AND CHOPPED

1/3 CUP CHOPPED ONION

1/4 CUP PICANTE SAUCE OR SALSA

1/4 TSPS SALT

THIN GUACAMOLE

	SERVES: 5	**TOTAL TIME: 10 MIN**
	10	

DIRECTIONS:

Place the onion, jalapeño, salt and half the coriander on a cutting board and use a fork to mash until juicy. OR do this in a mortar and pestle – grind into a paste.

Scrape into a bowl, add avocado and remaining coriander, and mash to desired consistency. Do the taste test and then adjust it to your taste: salt, lime juice for sour, more chili for spiciness. If using tomatoes, stir through. Serve with corn chips!

INGREDIENTS:

2 TBSPS. FINELY CHOPPED WHITE ONION (OR RED, BROWN OR YELLOW)

1 TBSP. FINELY CHOPPED JALAPENO OR SERRANO CHILI (OR OTHER CHILI OF CHOICE) (ADJUST TO TASTE)

1/2 TSPS. SALT, PLUS MORE TO TASTE

1/4 CUP ROUGHLY CHOPPED CORIANDER/CILANTRO LEAVES

2 MEDIUM AVOCADOS (OR 1 VERY LARGE ONE) (NOTE 1)

LIME JUICE, TO TASTE (I USE 1/4 – 1/2 LIME)

OPTIONAL: 1-2 RIPE TOMATOES, PEELED, DESEEDED AND CHOPPED

CREAMY GUACAMOLE

SERVES: 8	TOTAL TIME: 6 MIN
11	

DIRECTIONS:

Place the pulp from the avocados in a medium bowl and slightly mash with a fork or a potato masher leaving some large chunks. Add lime juice, salt, pepper, cilantro, red onion, garlic and mix thoroughly.

If you are serving this at a later time, a great tip to keep the guacamole from turning brown is to cover tightly with plastic wrap so no air gets on it. Make 2 cups.

INGREDIENTS:

15 OZ. FROM 3 MEDIUM HASS PITTED AND HALVED AVOCADOS

1 LIME, JUICED

1/3 CUP RED ONION, MINCED

1 SMALL CLOVE GARLIC, MASHED

1 TBSP. CHOPPED CILANTRO

KOSHER SALT AND FRESH PEPPER, TO TASTE

CHAPTER 4

Appetizer & Sides

AVOCADO MEATBALLS AND LENTILS

	SERVES: 4	TOTAL TIME: 1H 30 MIN
	12	

DIRECTIONS:

Peel the avocado and cut the pulp into small pieces.

Blend the avocado pulp together with half of the lentils, part of the nuts, the breadcrumbs and then adjust with salt and curry.

We take hollow oval shapes, grease them with oil and fill them with the mixture. Or, if we do not have the molds, we lay the mixture on greased baking paper and with a glass form circles to compose the meatballs.

Spread 1 sheet of baking paper on the baking tray and bake the meatballs.

Leave to cook for about 20 minutes at 356°F, until they form a crust.

Serve garnished with crumbled walnut pieces.

INGREDIENTS:

15 OZ. COOKED LENTILS

2 OZ. BREADCRUMBS OR STALE

½ AVOCADO

1 OZ. WALNUTS

¼ TSP. SALE

½ TSP. CURRY POWDER

AVOCADO TARTAR AND ZUCCHINI

SERVES: 4	**TOTAL TIME: 30 MIN**

13

DIRECTIONS:

Cut into cubes: courgettes, avocado and onion and mix in a bowl, adding oil and lemon juice. Leave to marinate for 1h.

Taste to adjust the amount of salt and sprinkle with ginger.

Serve with bread croutons on the side.

INGREDIENTS:

2 AVOCADOS

2 COURGETTES

1 RED ONION

1 LEMON

1 TBSP. GINGER POWDER

1 TBSP. EXTRA VIRGIN OLIVE OIL

¼ SALT AND PEPPER

PUMPKIN AND AVOCADO SKEWERS

SERVES: 4	TOTAL TIME: 30 MIN
14	

DIRECTIONS:

Clean the pumpkin and remove the peel, seeds and internal filaments, then cut it into regular cubes. Place the pumpkin cubes on a lined plate and bake at 356°F for about 20-25 minutes. When the pumpkin has formed a crispy golden crust on the surface and will be soft inside, remove it from the oven.

Clean the avocado and remove the central seed then cut into pieces, then sprinkle with a few drops of lemon juice. Prepare a sauce with extra virgin olive oil, salt, pepper, chopped herbs and chili. Skewer the pumpkin and avocado alternating and then sprinkle with the aromatic sauce.

INGREDIENTS:

18 OZ. PUMPKIN

2 AVOCADOS

1 TBSP. EXTRA VIRGIN OLIVE OIL

1 TBSP. MIXED AROMATIC HERBS: SAGE, ROSE MARY, THYME

1 TBSP. CHILI

1/8 TSP. SALT AND PEPPER

ZUCCHINI & AVOCADO ROLLS

	SERVES: 4	TOTAL TIME: 40 MIN
	15	

DIRECTIONS:

Wash and dry the zucchini, remove the ends and cut into slices in the direction of length. Steam them for about 2 minutes, then lay them on a clean kitchen towel. Pat dry and transfer to a sheet of baking paper.

Cut the avocado in half and remove the core, remove the pulp with a Tsp and blend it together with lemon juice, salt and pepper.

Spread the avocado puree on the zucchini slices and roll them softly.

Spread the rolls externally with ricotta cheese.

Roll the rolls in sesame seeds and place on a tray.

Sprinkle with chili pepper and serve.

INGREDIENTS:

2 COURGETTES

2 AVOCADOS

1 TBSP. LEMON JUICE

3 TSPS. RICOTTA CHEESE

3 TBSPS. SESAME

1 TBSP. EXTRA VIRGIN OLIVE OIL

¼ TSP. SALT AND PEPPER

PEPPERS AND AVOCADO OMELETTE

SERVES: 2

16

TOTAL TIME: 35 MIN

DIRECTIONS:

Cut the avocado in half, cut the pulp and cut into cubes. Set aside by spraying it with lime juice to prevent it from blackening.

Clean and cut the red pepper into strips and cut the onion into rounds.

In a pan put the extra virgin olive oil and butter, when the butter has melted, sauté the onion.

Add the strips of peppers and cook for at least 10 minutes.

Break and beat the eggs with a fork in a bowl with salt and pepper.

Pour the beaten eggs into the pan with the pumpkin, use a wooden fork to cook the omelet evenly.

INGREDIENTS:

1 RED PEPPER

1 ONION

3 EGGS

1 AVOCADO

1 LIME

1 TBSP. BUTTER

1 TBSP. EXTRA VIRGIN OLIVE OIL

¼ SALT AND BLACK PEPPER

40

Add the avocado cubes evenly.

Cover with a lid and cook over a moderate heat until the omelet is cooked over.

Serve hot.

AVOCADOS' SMOKED SALMON IN LIME AND SOY SAUCE

SERVES: 4

17

TOTAL TIME: 30 MIN

DIRECTIONS:

Spread the smoked salmon slices in a large tray with slightly raised edges

Peel the avocado, split it in two and remove the core then cut into small pieces

Place the pieces of avocado on the salmon

Prepare a mixture with lime juice, soy sauce and extra virgin olive oil, mix well and sprinkle with this sauce salmon and avocado

Finish with a generous sprinkling of black pepper and serve

INGREDIENTS:

6 OZ. SLICED SMOKED SALMON

2 AVOCADOS

1 LIME

T TBSP. EXTRA VIRGIN OLIVE OIL

1 TBSP. SOY SAUCE

½ TSP. BLACK PEPPER

AVOCADO PUDDING WITH CRAB

SERVES: 4	TOTAL TIME: 30 MIN
18	

DIRECTIONS:

Blend the pulp of the avocado with the vegetable broth, 2 egg whites, the spoon of soy sauce, salt and pepper.

Spread the crab pulp on the bottom of 4 heat-resistant glasses and cover with the prepared cream. Steam for 10 minutes, then cool in the refrigerator.

Dice the tomato and cucumber and garnish the glasses.

Sear the shrimp in a pan.

Add a few mint leaves and a shrimp to each glass.

Serve the puddings cold.

INGREDIENTS:

1 AVOCADO

7 OZ. CRABMEAT

¼ CUP VEGETABLE BROTH

2 EGG WHITES

½ AND CUCUMBER

1 TOMATO

4 SHRIMP

1 TBSP. SOY SAUCE

1 TSP. LEMON JUICE

1 BUNCH OF MINT

¼ TSP. SALT AND PEPPER

AVOCADO ROLLS WITH SALMON & KUMQUAT

SERVES: 10	TOTAL TIME: 50 MIN
19	

DIRECTIONS:

Spike the kumquats with a toothpick and dip in warm water for 2-3 hours to lose some of the bitter taste.

Whip the soft butter until foamy and incorporate the pulp of the avocado blend quickly at the last minute with a hand blender. Put the pepper and add a little salt if necessary.

Lay the 2 slices of bread with the rolling pin on an aluminum foil, slightly overlapping them on the long side. Spread the prepared avocado mixture, then cover with slices of salmon and roll. Seal the roll in aluminum foil and put it in the freezer for 2 hours.

Drain the kumquats, cut them in half and cook for about ten minutes in a saucepan with a cup of water, sugar and rosemary.

Remove the avocado and salmon

INGREDIENTS:

1-2 AVOCADOS

3 TBSPS. SALTED BUTTER

3 TSPS. SUGAR

7 OZ. SMOKED SALMON

20 KUMQUATS

1 SPRIG OF ROSEMARY

2 SLICES OF BREAD FOR SANDWICHES

1 TSP. SALT AND PEPPER

roll from the freezer and remove the aluminum, then cut it into 1 cm slices with a sharp knife and leave them at room temperature for a few minutes before serving with warm candied kumquats.

PASTA SALAD WITH AVOCADO AND LIME

SERVES: 4	TOTAL TIME: 25 MIN

20

DIRECTIONS:

Boil the pasta, an ideal format are the shells, in boiling salted water. Drain al dente and put them under cold water to stop cooking.

Peel the avocado, cut it into cubes and baste with lemon juice. Dice the tomatoes, peel the lime and then cut into slices.

Mix the boiled cold pasta shells with the seasoned avocado, the diced tomatoes, the sliced lime, the drained tuna in oil, salt, pepper, oil and oregano.

Serve pasta salad with avocado and lime on top.

INGREDIENTS:

12 OZ. DURUM WHEAT SEMOLINA PASTE (SHELL-SHAPED)

1 CUP CANNED TUNA IN OIL

1 AVOCADO

1 LIME

2 TOMATOES

1 TSP. LEMON JUICE

1 TBSP. OLIVE OIL

1 TSP. OREGANO

½ TSP. SALT AND PEPPER

CHAPTER 5

SALADS, SOUPS & SANDWICHES

WARM SALAD WITH PUMPKIN AND AVOCADO

SERVES: 3	TOTAL TIME: 35 MIN
21	

DIRECTIONS:

Finely chop the leek, add a chopped chives, parsley, dried mint and whole dried chili pepper (so you can remove it towards the end of cooking): in a spoonful of oil lightly fry the aromas and then add, the chopped pumpkin, the apple vinegar and the agave syrup. Add salt and if necessary a Tbsp. of hot water or vegetable broth.

When the pulp of the pumpkin becomes tender, remove the chili pepper and add the previously boiled spelt: let the cereal flavor well with the seasoning.

Cut the avocado into small pieces and sprinkle with lemon juice. On low heat add the avocado to the pumpkin and mix everything. Serve immediately.

INGREDIENTS:

1 CUP SPELT

11 OZ. PUMPKIN

1 AVOCADO

1 LEMON JUICE

1 TBSP. LEEK

1 TBSP. CHIVES

1 BUNCH OF PARSLEY

1 BUNCH OF MINT

1/8 TSP. CHILI POWDER

1 TBSP. APPLE VINEGAR

1 TBSP. AGAVE SYRUP

1 TBSP. EXTRA VIRGIN OLIVE OIL

1/8 TSP. SALT

TURKEY RUMP AND AVOCADO SANDWICHES

	SERVES: 4	TOTAL TIME: 10 MIN
	22	

DIRECTIONS:

Wash, peel and cube the avocado.

In a chopper, add the avocado cubes, the cream cheese, a pinch of salt and lemon juice. Reduce everything into cream.

Take a slice of bread for sandwiches and spread a layer of avocado cream with a knife.

Add the slices of turkey breast and close with a second slice of bread.

Repeat until all ingredients are used up.

Cut each sandwich in a triangle and serve.

INGREDIENTS:

9 OZ. SANDWICH BREAD

4 OZ. TURKEY BREAST

1 AVOCADO

2 TBSPS. SPREADABLE CHEESE

½ LEMON JUICE

1/8 TSP. SALT

CHICKEN SOUP AND AVOCADO

	SERVES: 4	TOTAL TIME: 30 MIN
	23	

DIRECTIONS:

Cut the chicken breast into slices, rinse and pat dry with paper towels.

Slice very finely the peeled onion and the 3 cloves of garlic peeled and put everything to fry in a pan with high edges with extra virgin olive oil and chopped chili pepper.

Brown for 3 minutes, then add the chicken breasts cut into strips and fry for 10 minutes over high heat.

When the meat is well sealed, add the tomato

INGREDIENTS:

26 OZ. CHICKEN BREAST

1 ONION

2 AVOCADOS

2 TBSPS. TOMATO CONCENTRATE

3 CLOVES OF GARLIC

1 CHOPPED CHILI PEPPER

1 TBSP. EXTRA VIRGIN OLIVE OIL

18 OZ. CHICKEN BROTH

¼ TBSP. SALT AND PEPPER

paste, chicken broth and bring it to a boil, then salt and pepper and cook for 40 minutes, stirring occasionally, lowering the heat and covering with the lid.

At 5 minutes from the end of cooking, peel the avocados and cut them in half, remove the seed inside, then cut into wedges and add them in the pot.

Finish the preparation so that the slices of fruit soften, then turn off the heat and serve the soup hot.

	SERVES: 4	TOTAL TIME: 35 MIN
AVOCADO SOUP AND YOGURT	24	

DIRECTIONS:	INGREDIENTS:
Peel the avocados, remove the core, cut the pulp into cubes to be put in a bowl and sprinkle with lemon juice. Pour over the yogurt and stir. Put everything in the blender and blend several times, adding the broth. Pour the mixture into a bowl, season with salt and pepper and let cool in the refrigerator. Serve the soup with chives over to garnish.	**4** AVOCADOS **1** CUP OF VEGETABLE BROTH **1** CUP NATURAL YOGURT **1** LEMON **1** TBSP. CHIVES **¼** TSP. SALT AND PEPPER

AVOCADO CREAM WITH SMOKED SALMON

SERVES: 4	TOTAL TIME: 20 MIN
25	

DIRECTIONS:

Cut the avocado in half lengthwise, remove the stone and blend most of the pulp with lemon juice and cream. Save some avocado cubes for decoration.

Place the cream in a bowl and add salt and pepper and let stand for 10 minutes.

Slice the smoked salmon.

Put the avocado cream in 3-4 plates and serve with the smoked salmon inside. Add the whipped cream, the remaining avocado cubes and chives to the center as a decoration.

INGREDIENTS:

1 AVOCADO

1 LEMON

2 TBSPS. KITCHEN CREAM

7 OZ. SMOKED SALMON

¼ CUP WHIPPED CREAM

¼ TSP. SALT AND PEPPER

1 TSP. CHIVES

VELVET OF AVOCADO

SERVES: 4	TOTAL TIME: 15 MIN

26

DIRECTIONS:

Peel the avocados, cut into slices and put them in the mixer, chopping them together with lemon juice and salt.

Blend for a minute then add the broth and blend again until the mixture becomes smooth and homogeneous.

Pour into a bowl and dilute with yogurt.

Cover the bowls and keep them in the fridge for a couple of hours.

Distribute the velvet in four holsters and sprinkle the surface with the white part of the spring onions cut into rings.

INGREDIENTS:

2 AVOCADOS

1 CUP FAT FREE BOUILLON

1 CUP NATURAL YOGURT

2 SPRING ONIONS

2 TSPS. LEMON JUICE

CASHEW SALAD, AVOCADO AND TURKEY BREAST

SERVES: 4	TOTAL TIME: 15 MIN
27	

DIRECTIONS:

Prepare dressing in a bowl by combining Tabasco sauce, yogurt, salt, pepper, olive oil.

Mix the salad with the radicchio, avocado, cashews and Turkey Breast Petals.

Season with the Tabasco sauce dressing and serve.

INGREDIENTS:

3 OZ TURKEY BREAST ALREADY COOKED

1/3 CUP OF CASHEWS

1 CUP RED RADISH

1 CUP SPINACH

1 CUP YOGURT

1 TBSP. LEMON JUICE

1 TBSP. EXTRA VIRGIN OLIVE OIL

¼ TSP SALT AND PEPPER

¼ TSP TABASCO SAUCE

POMEGRANATE TURKEY WITH AVOCADO

SERVES: 4	TOTAL TIME: 30 MIN
28	

DIRECTIONS:

Cut the avocados in half lengthwise, remove the stones and the skin.

Cut the pomegranate in two, put it facing with the grains towards a bowl and beat it firmly on the side of the skin to extract all the grains (to help you use a spoonful stiff).

Take a quarter of the grains and pour it (or better centrifuge) to get the juice.

Mix the oil with the pomegranate juice, add the mustard, season with salt and pepper and stir.

Pass the chicken breasts on a hot plate for about 4 minutes on each side.

Then cut them into morsels.

Place the morsels in a plate, garnish with pomegranate beans and avocado pieces, sprinkle everything with the sauce and serve.

INGREDIENTS:

2 TURKEY BREASTS

1 POMEGRANATE

2 AVOCADOS

2 TBSPS. EXTRA VIRGIN OLIVE OIL

½ TBSP. OF SWEET MUSTARD

¼ SALT AND PEPPER

MEDITERRAN EAN SALAD

SERVES:	TOTAL TIME: 10 MIN
2	
29	

DIRECTIONS:

Preparing the Mediterranean salad is very easy.

First of all we prepare the vinaigrette: in a bowl beat with a fork, the oil with one of vinegar and a pinch of salt.

Put just a few salt because the feta is already very salty. You will always have time to add later.

Emulsify with a fork until you see that the two ingredients form an almost dense compound.

Let it rest and take a large bowl where you will put the salad already washed and dried.

If the leaves are not large, leave them whole.

Add the chopped tomatoes, the pitted black olives, 3 Tbsps of extra virgin olive oil, a Tbsp of vinegar

INGREDIENTS:

8 OZ. ROCKET SALAD OR VALERIAN

1 AVOCADO

2 TBSPS. GREEK FETA CHEESE

6 RIPE TOMATOES

10 BLACK OLIVES

3 TBSPS. EXTRA VIRGIN OLIVE OIL

1 TBSP. BALSAMIC VINEGAR

¼ TSP. SALT AND PEPPER

and stir.

Now crumble over the cheese and finally add the avocado peeled and cut into slices, sprinkle with a little lemon juice to prevent it from darkening.

Mix everything gently and serve your delicious summer salad with toasted bread croutons.

AVOCADO SALAD WITH FETA & WALNUTS

SERVES: 2-3	TOTAL TIME: 10 MIN
30	

DIRECTIONS:

Clean the salad: break the leaves with your hands and wash them carefully in a centrifuge.

Shell the nuts and pound them in a mortar. Decide how much to insist on according to your taste, but do not pound them too much or you will only get a powder.

Peel the avocado, remove the stone and cut into strips. To prevent it from blackening, sprinkle with lemon.

Cut the feta into strips as big as the avocado slices.

Make the dish: place under the salad and on top alternate a slice of feta with one of avocado. Over, sprinkle the crumbled nuts.

Season it with olive oil and salt only when eating salad.

INGREDIENTS:

8 OZ. GREEN LETTUCE SALAD

7 OZ. GREEK FETA CHEESE

5 NUTS

1 AVOCADO

1 LEMON JUICE

1 TBSP. OLIVE OIL

AVOCADO SALAD WITH FETA & CUCUMBERS

	SERVES: 4	TOTAL TIME: 30 MIN
	31	

DIRECTIONS:

Remove the peel from the cucumbers and cut into thin slices.

Cut the feta into cubes.

Remove the peel from the avocado, remove the stone and sprinkle the avocado with the juice of half a lemon, then cut into pieces. Split the olives in half.

Mix the remaining lemon juice with about 2-3 tbsps. of oil and finely chopped mint. Pour all the ingredients into a large bowl and season with the mint emulsion. Serve immediately.

INGREDIENTS:

14 OZ. CUCUMBERS

7 OZ. GREEK FETA CHEESE

3 OZ. LETTUCE SALAD

1 AVOCADO

1 LEMON

1 SPRIG OF MINT

2 TBSPS. BLACK OLIVES

1 TBSP. EXTRA VIRGIN OLIVE OIL

AVOCADO SALAD WITH FETA & ORANGE

SERVES: 4

32

TOTAL TIME: 20 MIN

DIRECTIONS:

Remove the orange peel and the inner white parts, then cut them into rounds or slices and leave them aside.

Cut the avocado in half, remove the peel, the seed inside and scoop out the pulp with a spoon. Cut the pulp into cubes.

Make up the salad: the orange slices will make the first layer, then put the avocado cubes, then crumble the Greek feta and over the mixed buds and roughly cut walnuts.

Season with oil, salt, pepper and serve immediately.

INGREDIENTS:

3 ORANGES

1 AVOCADO

3 OZ. GREEK FETA CHEESE

2 TBSPS. WALNUTS

1 TBSP. MIXED SPROUTS

1 TBSP. EXTRA VIRGIN OLIVE OIL

¼ TSP. SALT AND PEPPER

	SERVES: 4	TOTAL TIME: 20 MIN
TOMATOES CHILI ONIONS & AVOCADO	33	

DIRECTIONS:

Peel the avocado, cut it into thin slices and bowl it with lemon juice.

Cut the green lemon into slices, then place on a plate and add salt.

Crush the garlic with a fork and collect the cream obtained in a bowl, add 6 tbsps. of oil, a Tbsp. of parsley and the chili pepper finely chopped with pistachios. Add salt and add the tomatoes you cut into cubes.

Cut the white part of the spring onions into thin slices and immerse them in water and ice for 10 minutes.

Now pass under running water the green lemon, remove the liquid from the spring onions and mix all in a bowl with the avocado drained.

Add avocado lemon juice to the dressing, mix well and enjoy with the guests.

INGREDIENTS:

2 AVOCADOS

2 SPRING ONIONS

2 SALAD TOMATOES

1 CHILI PEPPER

1 LIME

2 TBSPS. FRESH PISTACHIOS

1 BUNCH OF PARSLEY

1 CLOVE OF GARLIC

1 TBSP. EXTRA VIRGIN OLIVE OIL

¼ TSP. SALE

CARROT, APPLE & AVOCADO SALAD

	SERVES: 6	TOTAL TIME: 15 MIN
	34	

DIRECTIONS:

Begin with the salad by removing the kale from the ribs. The ribs are too tough to eat in salads like this, but you can save them to sauté for sides or stir fry's later if you want to reduce the waste.

Once the ribs are removed chop your kale into bite sized pieces Transfer the kale to a large salad bowl and sprinkle with a pinch of salt. Drizzle 1 Tbsp. of olive oil over the leaves and begin scrunching the leaves until they become darker in color. You'll feel the leaves become softer as your rub - this should only take about 30 seconds.

Next you need to dry fry your Halloumi. Slice the cheese as thin/thick as you'd like. Warm a skillet on a medium heat and lay the Halloumi out on the frying pan. Use a little bit of oil if you're using a cast iron, but you don't need to if you're using a non-stick pan. Let the

INGREDIENTS:

2 VERY LARGE BUNCHES OF KALE

PINCH OF SEA SALT

1 TBSP. EXTRA-VIRGIN OLIVE OIL

8 OUNCES HALLOUMI

2 HONEY CRISP APPLES, DICED

2 LARGE CARROTS, CHOPPED

1/4 CUP PUMPKIN SEEDS

1 AVOCADO

DRESSING

1/4 CUP ALMOND BUTTER

cheese toast in the pan for 2-3 minutes without stirring. Once it's turned golden on one side flip it over and repeat on the other side.

Once toasted, transfer the cheese to a cutting board and chop it up into little pieces before adding it the kale along with the remaining salad ingredients.

In a small jar add everything needed for the dressing and stir together until combined. Drizzle the dressing over the salad and toss well to combine.

2 TBSPS. OLIVE OIL

2 TBSPS. FRESHLY SQUEEZED LEMON JUICE

1 TBSPS. WATER

1 TBSP. DIJON MUSTARD

1 TBSP. RAW HONEY

¼ TSP. SALT, MORE TO TASTE

½ TSP. GARLIC

AVOCADO & ARTICHOKES TOAST

SERVES: 2-4	TOTAL TIME: 2H
35	

DIRECTIONS:

Fill a medium bowl with water and add the juice of ¼ of the lemon. Slice the rest of the lemon into wedges. Reserve one wedge for later, and add the remaining lemon wedges to the water. Transfer the artichokes to the lemon water as you work. Cut off the top quarter of the artichokes, about 1 inch. Remove and discard the first 3 to 4 layers of dark green outer leaves. Trim the stems to ½ inch, and then use a paring knife to peel away the woody part of the stems. Slice the artichokes in half lengthwise. Use a small spoon to remove the fuzzy choke from each half. Leave the artichokes in the lemon water until you're ready to use them.

Preheat the oven to 375°F. Brush a medium baking pan with ½ Tbsp of olive oil. Drain the artichokes and lemons, and then add them to the pan with the remaining ½ Tbsp of olive oil and generous pinches of salt and pepper. Gently toss with

INGREDIENTS:

1 LEMON

4-6 FRESH BABY ARTICHOKES

1 TBSP. EXTRA-VIRGIN OLIVE OIL, PLUS MORE FOR DRIZZLING

4 SLICES WHOLE-GRAIN BREAD (*SEE NOTE)

½ SMALL GARLIC CLOVE

1 SMALL AVOCADO

1 SCALLION, DICED

2 RED RADISHES AND/OR 1 SMALL WATERMELON RADISH, THINLY SLICED

2 TBSPS CHOPPED DILL

1 TBSP HEMP SEEDS, OPTIONAL

SEA SALT AND FRESHLY

your hands to coat evenly. Cover with foil and bake 20 to 30 minutes, or until the leaves are tender and the cut sides are nicely browned.

Meanwhile, place the bread on a baking sheet and drizzle with olive oil.

Bake it10 or 12 minutes until toasted. Remove from the oven and rub each piece with the cut side of the garlic clove.

Slice the avocado in half lengthwise and remove the pit. While the avocado is still in its shell, slice the flesh of both halves horizontally and vertically into cubes. Use the remaining lemon wedge to squeeze juice on each half and top with a pinch of salt. Scoop the seasoned avocado onto the toasts and mash it with the back of a fork. Top the toasts with the scallions, 1 or 2 artichoke halves, sliced radishes, dill and hemp seeds, if desired.

Season it to taste with salt and serve with the roasted lemons.

GROUND BLACK PEPPER

AVOCADO BRUSCHETTA

SERVES: 4-6	TOTAL TIME: 15 MIN
36	

DIRECTIONS:

Toss tomatoes in a small bowl with olive oil, white balsamic, minced garlic, salt and pepper.

To that add the peaches, avocado, basil and mint and toss to coat. Taste and adjust seasonings, adding more salt and pepper as needed.

Toast slices of bread and pile everything on top. Drizzle with more olive oil and serve immediately.

INGREDIENTS:

1 CUP SLICED CHERRY TOMATOES

DRIZZLE OF OLIVE OIL

1 GARLIC CLOVE, MINCED

DRIZZLE OF WHITE BALSAMIC VINEGAR

2-4 PEACHES, CUT INTO SMALL PIECES

1 AVOCADO, DICED

CHOPPED BASIL AND/OR MINT

½ TSP. SALT & PEPPER

ABOUT 4 - 6 SLICES OF BREAD

CHAPTER 6

MAINS

CHICKEN MARINADE

	SERVES: 6	TOTAL TIME: 40 MIN
	37	

DIRECTIONS:

In a bowl, stir together oil, lemon juice, soy sauce, balsamic vinegar, brown sugar, Worcestershire sauce, garlic, salt, and pepper.

Pierce chicken breasts with a fork all over. Place in a large Ziploc bag. Pour marinade over chicken.

Let marinate for at least 30 minutes. 4 - 5 hours is ideal.

Preheat grill to medium heat. Brush grill with oil to prevent sticking.

Place chicken on the grill. Cook for approximately 5 - 6 minutes per side, depending on the thickness of chicken. The internal temperature of the chicken should reach 165 degrees.

Remove chicken from grill and let rest for 5 minutes.

INGREDIENTS:

2 LBS. CHICKEN BREASTS TENDERS, OR THIGHS

1/3 - 1/2 CUP EXTRA VIRGIN OLIVE OIL DEPENDING ON PREFERENCE

3 TBSPS. FRESH LEMON JUICE

3 TBSPS. SOY SAUCE

2 TBSPS. BALSAMIC VINEGAR

1/4 CUP BROWN SUGAR

1 TBSP. WORCESTERSHIRE SAUCE

3 GARLIC CLOVES MINCED OR 1/2 TSPS. GARLIC POWDER

1 1/2 TSPS. SALT

1 TSP. PEPPER

GARNISH: FRESH PARSLEY

PASTA WITH AVOCADO

SERVES: 4

38

TOTAL TIME: 15 MIN

DIRECTIONS:

Start by taking care of the pasta: cook the spaghetti in a pot filled with lightly salted water to boil for the time indicated on the package.

In the meantime, take the pulp of a well-ripe Avocado Hass and put it in a mixer equipped with metal blades, add the creamy cheese Philadelphia, a generous pinch of salt and blend everything until you get a smooth and velvety cream.

As soon as the pasta is cooked, drain and season with the avocado cream, mix well, then serve your creamy avocado pasta on the table, ending with a grind of pepper and a bit of thyme leaves.

INGREDIENTS:

14 OZ. WHOLE SPAGHETTI

1 AVOCADO

2/3 CUP PHILADELPHIA CHEESE (CREAM)

1 BUNCH OF THYME LEAVES

¼ TSP. SALT AND PEPPER

71

FETTUCCINE WITH AVOCADO & PISTACHIOS

	Serves: 4	Total Time: 15 min
	39	13.

Directions:

Cook the pasta in abundant salted water, taking into account the cooking time indicated on the package.

While the pasta is cooking, we clean the avocados, remove the pulp with a spoon and put it in the glass of the blender by immersion.

Wash the leaves of the basil and without drying it we add it to the avocado, add salt, a Tbsp. of extra virgin olive oil and two tbsps. of cold water. Blend everything until it is in a velvety cream.

We heat a pan, add the previously chopped pistachios and shear them for a minute.

Drain the pasta al dente, put it inside a large pebble and add the avocado cream and a Tbsp of extra virgin olive oil, mix well and finish cooking in the

Ingredients:

12 OZ PASTA FETTUCCINE

2 AVOCADOS

1/3 CUP OF PEELED PISTACHIOS

2 TBSPS. EXTRA VIRGIN OLIVE OIL

1 BUNCH OF BASIL

1/8 TSP. PINK SALT

pan with the pistachios, adding a little to the cooking water. Cook for a minute then serve on the table with a sprinkling of pistachios.

SPAGHETTI WITH RICOTTA AVOCADO AND ALMONDS

SERVES: 4	TOTAL TIME: 20 MIN

40

DIRECTIONS:

Cut the avocado in half on the length side and remove the core.

Put the pulp in a low but wide pan and beat it with a fork.

Season it with oil and salt.

Cut the lime in half, press it to obtain the juice to put on the avocado pulp. Add the ricotta cheese.

In a small pan apart toast the chopped almonds.

In a saucepan boil slightly salted water and cook the pasta. At the end of cooking, store 1 cup of pasta cooking water.

INGREDIENTS:

9 OZ LARGE SPAGHETTI OR FETTUCCINE

1 CUP RICOTTA

1 AVOCADO

1 LEMON JUICE

1 TBSP. OLIVE OIL

2 TSPS. GRATED CHEESE

3 TBSPS. TOMATO SAUCE

1/8 CUP ALMOND GRAIN

¼ TSP. SALT AND PEPPER

When the pasta is almost ready, put it in the large pan together with the ricotta and avocado cream, add the grated cheese and stir. Cook lengthening with the water of the pasta to complete the cooking.

Put the pasta in the dishes and decorate each dish with pepper, tomato sauce and almond grains.

SPAGHETTI WITH SALMON AND AVOCADO

SERVES: 2	TOTAL TIME: 10 MIN

41

DIRECTIONS:

Put a pot of water on the fire, add a little salt and put a lid to speed up the boiling of the water.

Cut an avocado in half and peel half of avocado. Cut the avocado pulp into cubes.

Cut the salmon into thin strips, put the cut salmon in a bowl and cover with oil, half lemon juice and ginger powder. Add the avocado cubes and leave to marinate.

Pour the spaghetti into the pot over the heat with the water that should now boil and pour a tsp of oil.

INGREDIENTS:

7 OZ. SPAGHETTI

4 OZ. SALMON

½ AVOCADO

1 TSP. WITHOUT POWDER

½ TSP. SALT AND PEPPER

1 TBSP. OLIVE OIL

When the spaghetti is cooked, drain but leave them in the pot. Keep 2 cups of cooking water.

Add salmon and avocado, black pepper and some cooking water to the spaghetti. Light the fire and stir adding if needed, more cooking water until the dish is creamy.

Take the spaghetti with a fork and put them in the dish in the shape of a nest.

Serve with some pieces of avocado and salmon on top.

14. SAFFRON SPAGHETTI WITH ZUCCHINI AND AVOCADO	SERVES: 2	TOTAL TIME: 10 MIN
	42	

DIRECTIONS:	INGREDIENTS:
Cut the zucchini into julienne.	11 OZ. SPAGHETTI
Sauté the finely chopped onion and sauté the zucchini for a few minutes.	2 COURGETTES
Cook the spaghetti in plenty of salted water.	1 AVOCADO
Blend the avocado in a mixer with the lemon, salt, pepper and 1 sachet of saffron dissolved in 2 tbsps. of hot water.	2 SACHETS OF SAFFRON
	¼ SPRING ONION
	½ LEMON
Drain the pasta and sauté for 2/3 minutes in a pot with saffron to give it flavor.	1 TBSP. EXTRA VIRGIN OLIVE OIL
Season with the avocado cream and sautéed zucchini	1/8 SALT AND PEPPER

AVOCADO MAC & CHEESE

SERVES: 4	TOTAL TIME: 25 MIN
43	

DIRECTIONS:

Bring water to a boil in a large pot. Salt the water and add in macaroni.

Stir and cook until Al Dente, about 8-10 minutes. Drain and set aside.

While the pasta is cooking, make the avocado sauce by placing the garlic, avocados, lime juice, cilantro, salt and pepper into a food processor or blender.

Process it until smooth and creamy. Set aside.

To make the cheese sauce, place butter in a small saucepan and heat over medium heat. When butter is melted, whisk in flour to create a paste.

Whisk in milk until smooth. Stir with a wooden spoon until the sauce starts to thicken. Add in Pepper Jack cheese and stir until cheese is melted and sauce is creamy.

INGREDIENTS:

10 OUNCES DRY ELBOW MACARONI

2 CLOVES GARLIC MINCED

2 AVOCADOS PEELED AND PITTED

2 TBSPS. FRESH LIME JUICE

1/3 CUP CHOPPED FRESH CILANTRO

SALT AND PEPPER TO TASTE

2 TBSPS. BUTTER

2 TBSPS. ALL-PURPOSE FLOUR

1 CUP MILK

2 CUPS SHREDDED PEPPER JACK CHEESE

SALT AND PEPPER TO TASTE

FRESH AVOCADO CHUNKS

Place macaroni in a large bowl.

Pour the avocado sauce over the macaroni and stir until well coated. Add the cheese sauce and stir until macaroni is coated and creamy. Season it with salt and pepper, to taste.

Serve warm. Garnish with fresh avocado chunks, if desired.

FOR GARNISH, IF DESIRED

BEST SHAKSHUKA

SERVES: 4

44

TOTAL TIME: 35 MIN

DIRECTIONS:

Heat the oil over medium heat in a 12-inch lidded stainless steel or enamel-coated cast-iron skillet. Add the onion, red pepper, salt, and several grinds of fresh pepper and cook until the onion is soft and translucent, 6 to 8 minutes.

Reduce the heat to medium-low and add the garlic, paprika, cumin, and cayenne, if using. Stir and let cook for about 30 seconds, then add the tomatoes and Harissa paste. Simmer for 15 minutes until the sauce is

INGREDIENTS:

2 TBSPS. EXTRA-VIRGIN OLIVE OIL

1 CUP CHOPPED YELLOW ONION

1 RED BELL PEPPER, SEEDED AND DICED

¼ TSP. SEA SALT, MORE TO TASTE

FRESHLY GROUND BLACK PEPPER

3 MEDIUM GARLIC CLOVES, MINCED

thickened.

Add the spinach and stir until wilted. Make 3 to 5 wells in the sauce and crack in the eggs. Cover and cook until the eggs are set, 5 to 8 minutes. The timing will depend on how runny you like your egg yolks.

Season with salt and pepper to taste and sprinkle with the feta, parsley, avocado, and micro greens, if using. Serve with toasted bread for scooping.

½ TSP. SMOKED PAPRIKA

½ TSP. GROUND CUMIN

PINCH OF CAYENNE PEPPER, OPTIONAL

28 OZ. CAN CRUSHED TOMATOES

2 TBSPS. HARISSA PASTE, SEE NOTE

1 CUP FRESH SPINACH, CHOPPED

3 TO 5 EGGS

⅓ CUP CRUMBLED FETA CHEESE

¼ CUP FRESH PARSLEY LEAVES

1 AVOCADO, DICED

MICRO GREENS FOR GARNISH, OPTIONAL

TOASTED BREAD, FOR SERVING

WHOLE GREEN SPAGHETTI WITH CHICKPEAS

SERVES: 4	TOTAL TIME: 35 MIN
45	

DIRECTIONS:

Dry the chickpeas with kitchen paper. Place them in a bowl and add the flour. Mix well then put them in the baking tray lined with parchment paper. Cook the chickpeas for 20 minutes at 338°F.

Then put them in a strainer to completely eliminate excess flour. Place them in a small bowl and season with oil, salt, pink pepper and lime zest. Mix well.

In a pot pour the water and bring it to boil, then boil in the pasta.

In the meantime, cut the avocado lengthwise and remove the core. Collect the pulp with a spoon and

INGREDIENTS:

12 OZ. WHOLE WHEAT SPAGHETTI

2 AVOCADOS

2 TBSPS. LIME JUICE

1 ½ TBSP EXTRA VIRGIN OLIVE OIL

1 TSP. CHIVES

½ TSP. SALT

FOR THE CHICKPEAS:

9 OZ. PRECOOKED CHICKPEAS

1 TBSP. FLOUR 00

put it in a bowl to blend together with oil, salt and half lime juice. Finally add chives.

Drain the pasta and place in a large bowl, mix with oil and avocado cream. Serve the spaghetti and complete with the crispy chickpeas.

1 TBSP. EXTRA VIRGIN OLIVE OIL

½ TSP. SALT

½ TSP. PINK PEPPER

CHAPTER 7

DESSERTS

AVOCADO PUDDING AND PISTACHIOS

SERVES: 1	TOTAL TIME: 5 MIN
46	

DIRECTIONS:	INGREDIENTS:
Take a soft and ripe avocado, cut it in half, remove the core and with the help of a spoon remove it from the skin.

Blend the avocado with cocoa, honey and Greek yogurt until you get a smooth cream. Serve with pistachios. | ½ AVOCADO

1 TBSP. HONEY

2 TBSPS. BITTER COCOA

¾ WHITE GREEK YOGURT CUP

2 TBSPS. PISTACHIO GRANULES |

AVOCADO TART AND PISTACHIOS WITH BLUEBERRIES

SERVES: 6-8	TOTAL TIME: 40 MIN
47	

DIRECTIONS:

Blend the avocado pulp.Chop apart the pistachios. In a bowl, mix the flour, sugar, chopped pistachios, vanillin, and yeast, salt and lemon zest.

Add the pulp of the avocado and knead until the mixture is crumbled. Finally add the egg and knead again to have smooth and plastic dough.

If necessary add a little flour. Divide the dough into 2 parts so that one is a third of the other. Roll out the largest piece with a rolling pin and place in a buttered cake tin and floured.

Finish the edges with a knife and fill with jam. Roll out the other dough, cut into strips and make the classic crossings on the tart.

Bake in the oven at 356ºF for about 25 minutes.

INGREDIENTS:

1-2 AVOCADO

¼ CUP PISTACHIOS1 JAR OF BLUEBERRY JAM

9 OZ FLOUR

¾ CUP SUGAR

1 EGG

1/1 TSP BAKING POWDER

1 SACHET OF VANILLIN

1 LEMON

1/8 TSP SALT

15. AVOCADO PASTRY COOKIES	SERVES: 4	TOTAL TIME: 30 MIN
	48	

DIRECTIONS:	INGREDIENTS:
First, blend the avocado. Then work all the ingredients together for 15 minutes until you get compact and homogeneous dough. Cover with cling film and leave to rest in the refrigerator 30 minutes before use. Take the dough from the fridge and take the pieces of dough from the pastry to make small biscuits. Use cookie molds if you have six glasses upside down to shape cookies. Put the chocolate chips in the middle of each cookie. Continue until the pastry is finished. Bake the biscuits in the oven heated to 356°F for 15 minutes and serve.	11 OZ. FLOUR 00 4 OZ. SUGAR 1 AVOCADO 1 EGG ½ TBSP. BAKING POWDER FOR CAKES ½ LEMON FOR THE ZEST ½ VANILLA STICK 2 TBSPS.' DROPS OF CHOCOLATE

TOAST WITH AVOCADO AND STRAWBERRIES

SERVES: 4 PIECES

49

TOTAL TIME: 20 MIN

DIRECTIONS:

Set aside half a strawberry per slice of bread and dice the rest. Halve the avocado, pitted, remove the pulp from the skin and cut into slices.

Mix the honey with the lemon juice and mix with the strawberries and avocado.

Lightly toast the bread in a toaster.

Spread the yogurt on slices of bread and garnish with slices of avocado and strawberry cubes.

Sprinkle with the marinade of honey and lemon juice and decorate with the mint and strawberries set aside.

INGREDIENTS:

1 CUP STRAWBERRIES

1 AVOCADO

1 TBSP. LIQUID HONEY

2 TBSPS.' LEMON JUICE

4 SLICES OF WHOLE MEAL BREAD

6 OZ. NATURAL GREEK YOGURT

1 SPRIG OF MINT

CHAPTER 8

DRINKS

AVOCADO LEMON MINT SMOOTHIE

SERVES: 2

50

TOTAL TIME: 5 MIN

DIRECTIONS:

Remove the avocado flesh and add it to the blender jar.

Blend with all the other ingredients.

Taste and add more milk or honey if needed. Serve immediately in glasses.

INGREDIENTS:

2 AVOCADOS

1 TBSP. LEMON JUICE

6-7 FRESH MINT LEAVES

2 CUPS COLD MILK

2 TBSPS. HONEY

AVOCADO BANANA YOGURT LEMON SMOOTHIE

SERVES: 1-2

51

TOTAL TIME: 5 MIN

DIRECTIONS:

Combine everything in a blender and blend until smooth.

INGREDIENTS:

1/2 AVOCADO

1 FROZEN BANANA

1/4 CUP PLAIN YOGURT (I USED GREEK 0%)

JUICE OF HALF A LEMON

JUICE OF HALF AN ORANGE

1/2 TSPS. AGAVE

1/2 ALMOND MILK

1/4 CUP WATER

PINCH OF SALT

GOURMET COCKTAIL

SERVES: 4	TOTAL TIME: 20 MIN
52	

DIRECTIONS:

Peel the shrimp and set aside the head. Then, cut the pulp on the long side in half and discard the intestine. Alternatively if we bought some shrimp already cleaned we skip this step.

Brown a clove of garlic in a pan with plenty of extra virgin olive oil and after one or two minutes add the shrimp: cook over high heat and lightly blend with white wine, then add a little parsley and

INGREDIENTS:

8 SHRIMP

1 CLOVE OF GARLIC

1 CUP WHITE WINE

1 SPRIG OF PARSLEY

¾ CUP CREAMY CHEESE

½ TSP. CUMIN

½ TSP. OF CURRY

3 AVOCADOS

1 TBSP. OF OIL

½ CUP LEMON JUICE

remove from the heat.

To prepare the cream of avocado, cut the fruits in half and remove the stone, peel them and then cut them into large pieces to blend, add the extra virgin olive oil, lemon and orange juice, finally, salt and cumin..

Clean the tomatoes, removing all the seeds, cut them into small cubes and add them to the avocado cream.

Work the cream cheese putting a curry and mix well with the fork.

Serve the cocktail by placing in transparent cups a first layer of avocado cream, a second layer of cream cheese and, finally, two shrimps positioned so as to have the tail facing outwards.

½ CUP ORANGE JUICE

2 TOMATOES

AVOCADO NOG

SERVES: 2	TOTAL TIME: 5 MIN
53	

DIRECTIONS:

Put all avocado, banana, milk, vanilla extract, spice and bourbon in your blender. Mix until smooth. Sweeten to taste.

Pour eggnog into serving glasses, top with whipped topping and sprinkle with some grated nutmeg.

To serve: whipped topping, grated nutmeg.

INGREDIENTS:

1/2 AVOCADO

1/4 BANANA OPTIONAL

2 CUPS MILK COLD, DAIRY OR NON-DAIRY

1 TSP. VANILLA EXTRACT

1/4 - 1/2 TSPS. GINGERBREAD SPICE OR A PINCH OF NUTMEG

1 OUNCE BRANDY OR BOURBON

¼ TBSP

SWEETENER TO TASTE

AVOCADO BUBBLE TEA

SERVES: 2

54

TOTAL TIME: 15 MIN

DIRECTIONS:

Cook tapioca pearl according to the package instructions.

Strain it add honey.

Combine gently until the pearls are completely covered with honey. And Keep aside.

In the blender, add avocado, milk, condensed milk, and ice cubes.

Pulse until the mixture becomes smooth and silky.

In the serving glass, add a Tbsp. of tapioca pearls at the bottom.

Then add avocado mixture and the pearl alternatively for one or two times.

And Serve immediately.

INGREDIENTS:

1/4 CUP TAPIOCA PEARL/BOBA

2 TBSPS. HONEY TO SOAK THE TAPIOCA PEARLS

2 AVOCADO SOFT AND RIPEN

1 CUP MILK IN ROOM TEMPERATURE

2/3 CUP CONDENSED MILK /SUBSTITUTE WITH 4 TBSPS. OF SUGAR

1/2 CUP ICE CUBES

AVOCADO PIŇA COLADA

SERVES: 1

55

TOTAL TIME: 5 MIN

DIRECTIONS:

Place ingredients in the blender and blend, blend, blend.

Enjoy.

INGREDIENTS:

1 CUP GREENS

1/2 AVOCADO

1/2 CUP PINEAPPLE

1 TBSP. GROUND FLAXSEED

1/2 CUP V8 HEALTHY GREENS JUICE

1/2 CUP COCONUT YOGURT

16. AVOCADO & ANANAS COCKTAIL	SERVES: 1-2	TOTAL TIME: 5 MIN
	56	

DIRECTIONS:	INGREDIENTS:
Pour into the mixer the pineapple juice, brown sugar, half avocado and some ice cubes.	½ AVOCADO
	1 ½ CUP PINEAPPLE JUICE
Blend well all the ingredients, and then pour the mixture into an aperitif glass.	2 TBSPS. BROWN SUGAR
	1 TBSP. POMEGRANATE CHICHI
Garnish with julienne orange peel and some pomegranate.	1 ORANGE PEEL
	SOME ICE CUBE

AVOCADO DAIQUIRI

SERVES: 2-3	TOTAL TIME: 5 MIN
57	

DIRECTIONS:

Peel the avocados, cut into slices and put them in the mixer, chopping them together with lemon juice and salt.

Blend for a minute then add the broth and blend again until the mixture becomes smooth and homogeneous.

Pour into a bowl and dilute with yogurt.

Cover the bowls and keep them in the fridge for a couple of hours.

Distribute the velvet in four holsters and sprinkle the surface with the white part of the spring onions cut into rings.

INGREDIENTS:

2 AVOCADOS

1 CUP FAT FREE BOUILLON

1 CUP YOGURT NATURAL

2 CIPOLLOTTI

2 TSPS. LEMON JUICE

VELVET OF AVOCADO

	SERVES: 4	TOTAL TIME: 15 MIN
	58	

DIRECTIONS:	INGREDIENTS:
Mix the avocado with the rum, lemon juice and syrup. Then add the ice and stir until you get a uniform mixture (soft and creamy).	2 AVOCADOS 1 CUP FAT FREE BOUILLON 1 CUP YOGURT NATURAL 2 CIPOLLOTTI 2 TSPS. LEMON JUICE

CONCLUSION

Avocados are safe to eat for most people but may cause problems in individuals with allergy or IBS.

An allergy to avocado is rare, but individuals with a latex allergy can experience allergic reactions to fruits, such as avocados, bananas, or kiwis. According to an older study, this is known as a latex-fruit syndrome.

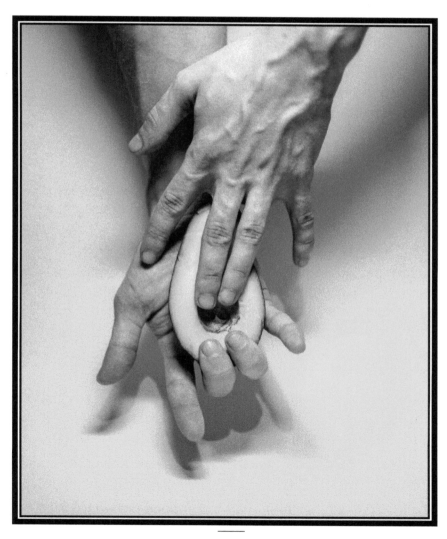

In latex-fruit syndrome, the immune system attacks fruit proteins similar to the allergy-causing proteins in the latex. This effect may lead to allergic reactions, including upset stomach, stomach cramps, headaches, or more severe symptoms, severe allergic shock.

Instead, symptoms of latex-avocado allergy include:

- swelling of the lips
- sneezing
- itchy eyes
- stomach discomfort, including vomiting

You also could have systemic reactions (such as hives) and an anaphylactic response (such as swelling of the airways and difficulty breathing), but a reaction this serious is sporadic from an avocado allergy. If it happens, call 911 or your local emergency services.

If you've been handling avocados and you feel symptoms of an allergic reaction on your skin, the pesticides and other crop chemicals on the surface of the avocado may be what's bothering you.

It might help to wash the avocado with a food-safe wash designed to remove chemicals. Choosing organic avocados, which haven't been exposed to chemicals, can also prevent this reaction.

There isn't a skin test for avocado allergy, but you might want to get a skin test for latex allergy.

If your symptoms aren't severe, an over-the-counter (OTC) antihistamine might make you feel more comfortable. If your skin is irritated, OTC cortisone cream may help.

However, the best way to avoid triggering an allergic reaction to avocados is to prevent them.

Shop for OTC antihistamines and cortisone creams.

Avocados don't just limit themselves to guacamole and California rolls. You can find them in all sorts of unexpected places. These places can include dishes where avocados might not seem like a likely ingredient.

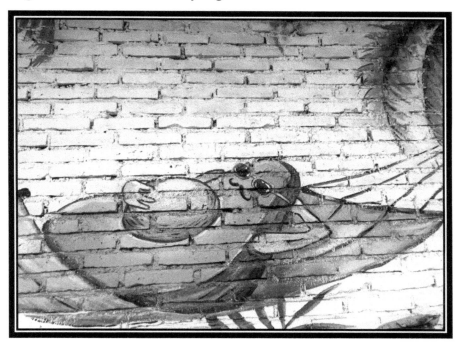

For example:

Vegan and paleo recipes sometimes use avocado to add creaminess since those diets avoid dairy products.

It's even used as a substitute for butter or other fats in some recipes.

In baked goods, avocado is said to provide a fluffy texture. It's even used in some chocolate chip cookie and brownie recipes.

Some cosmetics such as lotions and shampoos use avocado since its high-fat level adds to the moisturizing qualities of these products. A reaction to avocado used in cosmetics is unlikely, but check the ingredient list for avocados if you experience an allergic reaction.

If you suspect that you're allergic to avocados, see your doctor for allergy testing.

Allergy testing may reveal that you're allergic to latex as well. You could also discover that you don't have an actual avocado allergy but instead react to crop chemicals used in conventional or non-organic versions of the fruit.

If your doctor confirms that you have an avocado allergy, you'll have to be diligent about avoiding them. As a versatile food with a creamy texture, avocado may be "hiding" in your favourite dishes and desserts.

Avocado allergies are rarely severe, however. If you do accidentally eat the fruit, you'll likely be able to manage your symptoms with OTC oral medications or creams.

If you're an avocado lover and are disappointed to find yourself allergic, there are plenty of substitutes.

The most commonly recommended substitution is cooked (and cooled) chayote squash. Chayote squash doesn't have much flavour, so it mixes well with garlic, tomatoes, onion, and lime to make a delicious quasi-guacamole.

If it's the creamy green look you're after, try pureeing green peas for spreads or another fresh take on guacamole. Cooked, pureed asparagus and broccoli are similar substitutes, but they do have a much stronger flavour.

Try marinated, sliced hearts of palm or artichoke hearts to substitute for avocado's salty taste in salads or sandwiches.

THANK YOU

FOR CHOOSING MY COOKBOOK

AND TRYING OUT

MY HEALTHY AVOCADO'S RECIPES!

Aimie Lee

CPSIA information can be obtained
at www.ICGtesting.com
Printed in the USA
LVHW070215240621
691029LV00005B/204